THE WESTHILL PROJECT R.E. 5–16

CHRISTIANS

1

GARTH READ

JOHN RUDGE

ROGER B. HOWARTH

MARY GLASGOW PUBLICATIONS

Published by Mary Glasgow Publications Limited,
Avenue House, 131-133 Holland Park Avenue,
London W11 4UT.

© Mary Glasgow Publications Limited 1987

Designed by SNAP Graphics Ltd., London.
Phototypesetting in Great Britain by Franklyn
Graphics, Formby.
Printed in Great Britain by
W. S. Cowell Ltd, Ipswich.

British Library Cataloguing in Publication Data

Read, Garth
    Christians. — (The Westhill Project R.E. 5–16)
    1
    1. Christian biography — Juvenile literature
    I. Title   II. Rudge, John   III. Howarth,
    Roger B.   IV. Series
    209'.2'2   BR1704

    ISBN 0-86158-694-8

Acknowledgements

The authors and publishers are grateful to the following for permission to use copyright
material:

Photographs
Jerry Wooldridge cover top left, bottom right, pages 4, 6, 8, 9, 10, 12, 18, 19, 20, 21, 22, 26
top, 27 top, 30, 31, 32, 34, 36, 38 left, 39, 42, 54, 55, 58, 63 bottom;
The Sacred Trinity Centre, Manchester cover top right;
Daniel Lloyd, Boutcher Primary School, London SE1 cover bottom left;
Andy Coates page 5;
Church Missionary Society pages 24 top, 27 bottom;
Rachael Gregory page 38 right;
Sally and Richard Greenhill page 26 bottom;
Methodist Church Overseas Division page 24 bottom;
Ardea page 63 top.

Text
June Jones for the story on pages 14-17

The illustrations on pages 3, 14-15, 16-17, 23, 28, 37, 41 are by Sheila Faichney, on pages 25,
44-5, 46-7, 48-9, 50-1, 52-3, 56-7, 59, 60-1 by Jane Bottomley.

1 People

We all need other people.
Who did you need today?

Was it

Mummy?

Daddy?

a teacher?

a friend?

a lollipop man or woman?

STOP CHILDREN CROSSING

We need other people
   to be our friends,
   to help us,
   to share things with,
   to learn things from.

In your school you can find friends. You can help other people. You can share things. You can learn new things.

You can do lots of things at school because there are other people to help you.

Your school is a community.

Communities are groups of people who belong together and need each other.

People are not all the same.

Some people are big and some are small.
And some are short,
And some are tall;
And some are fat,
And some are thin;
With black or white or yellow skin.

People who are different can belong to the same
community.

Christians

Many people belong to Christian communities.

Christians are people who believe in Jesus Christ.

All Christians are not the same.

Some Christians are big and some are small;
And some are short,
And some are tall;
And some are fat,
And some are thin;
With black or white or yellow skin.

Christian communities are groups of people who
meet together because they believe in Jesus Christ.

Places where Christians meet

Christians like to meet together.

They have special places where they meet.

They have different names for the places where they meet.

church

chapel

meeting house

citadel

cathedral

See if you can find these words under the pictures on the next page.

church

chapel

meeting house

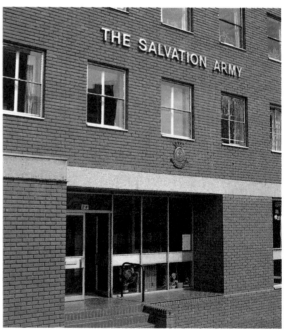

citadel

Yes, one name was missing.

Did you see which one it was?

Cathedrals are usually very big and beautiful places.

Lots of people can meet in a cathedral.

Cathedrals are usually in cities where there are crowds of people.

Most Christians use the name **church** for the place where they meet together.

Churches are not all the same.

Let us look inside one church.

There are lots of rows of seats. They look very hard and straight.

There are places for people to put their books and some soft cushions for them to kneel on.

The windows are very colourful. They are pictures which tell a story. The stories come from the Bible.

The Bible is a very special book for Christians.
It is on the stand that looks like a big eagle.
This stand is called a **lectern**.

On one side of the church there is a **pulpit**. This is like a large box with carvings on the outside. The ministers or priests go into it when they want to talk to the people.
It is high up so that everyone can see them.

At the far end of the church is a special table. It has a white cloth on it. It also has some candles and a cross on it. It is called an **altar**.

The people who meet in this church believe in Jesus Christ. They like lots of colour and music in their church. They also use pictures, statues and special furniture. The place where they meet is very different from their homes, schools or shops. It is a place of worship.

Let us look at another place where Christians meet.

This place is very different from the church.

It is called a **meeting house**.

There are no pictures and no special furniture.
The people in this meeting house sit in rows facing
each other.

The Christians who meet here are called Friends or
Quakers. They, too, believe in Jesus Christ.

They meet in very simple and plain buildings.

They like to be very quiet for a long time when they
meet together. While it is quiet and still they think about
God and about Jesus Christ.

This meeting house is also very different from homes,
schools and shops. It too is a place of worship.

Shanaz and Chetna visit a church

It was Jane's birthday. She was seven years old. As a treat her best friends, Shanaz and Chetna, went to her house for the day.

It was a Sunday and before the party and games, they all went to church with Jane's family.

'I've never been to a church before,' said Chetna. 'Is there anything that we must do?'

'No, I'll look after you,' said Jane. 'Mummy is telling the story in church this morning. Then we go to Sunday school. You can come with me.'

As they went into the church, Shanaz thought that it was not like a mosque. There were seats in rows. She wasn't used to that.

'We don't have seats in our mosque. Everybody sits on the floor,' she whispered to Chetna.

'We don't have seats in our temple either,' said Chetna. 'Isn't it funny?'

Lots of people said 'good morning' to the children as they found a seat.

Soon everybody was quiet as the minister came into the church and went into the pulpit.

After a short prayer, he told the people to stand and sing a song. The children had been given a book of songs by a man at the door. It was a very loud and lively song and everybody seemed to enjoy singing it.

'We call our songs ''hymns'',' Jane said to Chetna who was sitting next to her.

Soon a basket was passed along the rows of people and they put money into it.

Shanaz and Chetna hadn't brought any money and they were very worried.

Jane's father shook his head and said that it didn't matter a bit. 'Pass it to me,' said Jane.

Then Jane's mother went up to the front of the church to tell a story. She said that it was a story that Jesus had told many, many years ago.

Jane's mother was good at telling stories.

The story was about a man who was attacked by robbers. They wounded him and left him beside the road.

Some people saw him there, but they hurried past on the other side. At last one good man came along and he helped the injured man. He took him to an inn and even paid for him to be cared for.

After the story everybody sang another hymn. While it was being sung Jane, Shanaz and Chetna went with the other children to Sunday school.

They didn't like being in school again on a Sunday. However it was fun when they tried to tell the story of the robbers and the kind man. The teacher had brought some puppets to help them remember the story.

When it was over, Jane said, 'Come on Mummy. We want to go home and see my presents and have my party.'

Christians at worship

Shanaz and Chetna saw and heard many new things when they went to church with Jane.

Have you ever been to a church?

Perhaps you saw or heard some new things.

Can you remember some of them?

Christians worship God when they meet together in church.

Christians do many interesting things when they meet for worship.

Let's learn about some of them.

Singing

Many Christians sing hymns and songs when they worship God.

In some churches there are people who sing very well. When these people all sing together they are a choir. Sometimes the members of the choir wear brightly coloured gowns. Their singing helps other Christians to sing and to worship God.

In lots of churches all the people join in the singing.

Sometimes the singing is very loud and fast. Sometimes it is quiet and slow. Different kinds of music are used to worship God.

Some people stand and others sit when they sing their hymns.

Some people sway about, clap their hands or dance when they sing in their church.

Singing hymns helps Christians to worship God.

Praying

Praying is talking to God or thinking about God.

Sometimes it is hard to talk to someone you can't see or hear.

Christians believe that God can see and hear people. That's why they pray to God.

Sometimes the minister or priest says the prayers in church.

Sometimes all the people join together in saying the prayers.

Sometimes it is very quiet in church. People are talking to God in silence.

Christians believe that God listens to people's prayers.

That is why saying prayers is a special part of their worship.

Rituals

Rituals are special things that people do over and over again.

Christians do many special things when they worship.

Some of these they do again and again.

These rituals also help them to worship God.

Holy Communion

Holy Communion is an important ritual for most Christians. Bread and wine are used in this ritual.

The bread is on a special plate. It is called a **paten**.

The wine is in a special cup. It is called a **chalice**.

During the worship, people eat some of the bread and sip some of the wine.

For many Christians this is their most important ritual.

It has been done again and again for hundreds and hundreds of years.

Christians believe that Jesus started this ritual. At Holy Communion, they remember Jesus and believe he is with them.

Christians give money to their church.

Many do this during worship.

They put money on a plate, in a bag or in a basket.

The money is taken to the front of the church.

A minister or priest prays to God and puts the money on the altar.

This way of giving money is a ritual.

Most Christians give money every time they go to their church.

It too is a special way to worship God.

Some of this money is used to help other people.

Helping other people

In every community there are people who need help.

In every community there are people who give help to other people.

Have you helped anybody today?

Has anybody helped you today?

Perhaps you can talk to your friends and teachers about helping someone.

We can help people who are very busy.

We can help people who are very tired.

We can help people who are very old.

We can help people who are sad.

We can help people who are lonely.

We can help people who are sick.

We can help people who have no friends.

It is not always easy to help other people.

Sometimes we can't help the people we care about.
Someone else has to do it for us.

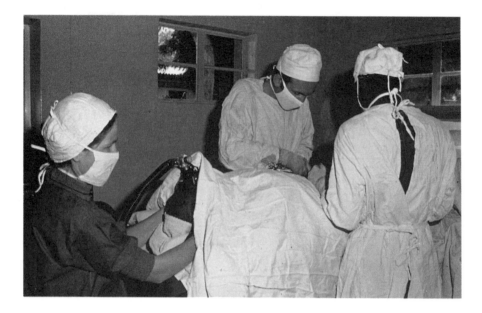

When people are very sick, doctors and nurses look after them for us.

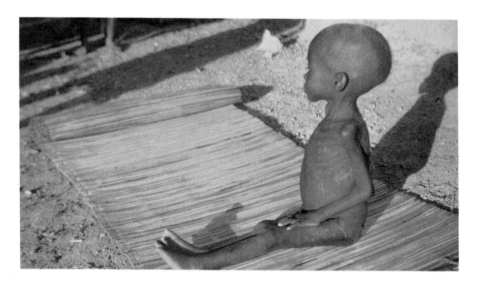

This little child is very hungry and sick. She cannot look after herself. Somebody else has to look after her.

When people in other countries are hungry and dying, other people look after them for us.

Christians helping other people

Lots of people help other people.

Christians help other people.

Christians believe that Jesus helped people.

Christians try to be like Jesus.

Here is a song which some Christian children sing in church to remind them that Jesus cared for people.

Jesus' hands were kind hands, doing good to all;
Healing pain and sickness, blessing children small;
Washing tired feet and saving those who fall;
Jesus' hands were kind hands, doing good to all.

Christians help all kinds of people.

Children who have no homes.
Old people who can't look after themselves.
Sick people who have to be in hospital.
People who can't find any work.
Poor people who have no money.
People who are lonely and frightened.

Some of the money which Christians give to their church
is used to help people.

Lots of people in our world need help. This man travelled from Africa to England to help people learn about his country.

This lady left her country to teach these children to read and write.
Some Christians travel to other countries to help people in need.
They do this because they believe that God loves all people, everywhere.

2 Families

We all belong to someone else.

Who do you belong to?

We belong to our fathers and mothers, brothers and sisters, uncles, aunts and cousins, grandfathers and grandmothers.

All these people are our family.

Some members of our family may have the same name as we do. It might be

Davies

or Macdonald

or Murphy

or Patel

or Rashid

or Smith.

Some members of our family may have different names from us.

Some members of our family may live in the same house as we do.

Some members of our family may live in other places.

Families are groups of people who belong to each other.

Welcoming babies

Sometimes a little baby is born into a family.

The new little baby belongs to the family.

Families are usually happy when a new baby is born.

They now have a new member in their family.

The baby must be given a name.

He or she must be given food, kept clean and warm and loved very much.

It is important to make the baby happy and feel welcome.

Christians welcoming babies

Christian families have special rituals or ceremonies for welcoming new babies.

Lots of friends may be invited to share in these ceremonies.

Christians have different names for these ceremonies.

These may sound funny if you have not heard them before.

Some Christians call their welcome ceremony **baptism**.

Others call their welcome ceremony **dedication and thanksgiving**.

In these ceremonies children are welcomed by their families and by the Christian community.

In the story on the next page you will read about how this cake was used by some Christians to say welcome to a little baby.

Michael's baptism ceremony

Michael is a very tiny baby. He is only six weeks old.

Michael's mother and father are Christians. They have brought little Michael to their church to be baptised.

The priest at the church is called Father David. He has a special part in this ritual.

Lots of other Christians are in the church. They want to say welcome to Michael too. They hope that as he grows up he will like belonging to their church.

The family gathers around a special stand near the back of the church. It is called a **font**. The top part is like a big bowl. There is water in this bowl.

Father David holds Michael in his arms. He asks Michael's mother and father to promise to help Michael to grow up as a Christian. He pours some water on Michael's head. He prays to God and asks him to look after Michael.

As Michael's mother and father take him back from Father David, they smile. They know that Michael is welcome in their family and in the Christian Church.

Someone has brought a special cake to church today. It has Michael's name on it. As everybody eats a piece they too know that Michael is welcome in their church.

Aaron's dedication and thanksgiving ceremony

Mr and Mrs Jones and their three children are Christians. Aaron is the baby of the family. He is two months old. His mother and father wanted to say thank you to God for their new baby. One Sunday they took Aaron to church for the service of dedication and thanksgiving.

The family sat together in the church during the morning worship. Their friends and other Christian families were there too.

Mr Brown, the minister, welcomed everybody and told them that this was a special day for little Aaron and his family. He then read a story from the Bible. The story was about Jesus welcoming some children and their mothers who came to talk to him. Jesus blessed the children by putting his hands on their heads.

Mr Brown then explained that Christians believe that God loves all people, especially little children.

Mr Brown then asked Mr and Mrs Jones if they would love and care for Aaron and teach him about God and Jesus. They said 'Yes'.

Mr Brown asked everyone in the church to stand up. While they were standing, they promised to help Aaron and his parents, brothers and sisters to be Christians.

Mr Brown then held Aaron high so everyone could see him. He prayed to God and asked God to bless Aaron and his family.

After the dedication and thanksgiving ceremony, many people spoke to the family and helped them to feel welcome in their church.

Baptism presents

Many Christians give a special present to the parents of the babies who are baptised in their church.

This beautiful candle is one of these presents.

It is lit just after the water is poured on the baby's head.

When Michael was baptised his parents received one of these candles.

Dedication and thanksgiving presents

A card was given to Aaron's parents after his dedication and thanksgiving ceremony.

Aaron's name is written on it.

Aaron's parents were also given a copy of the Bible to remind them of this special day.

Celebrating special days

Many families celebrate some important days each year.

'Celebrate' means to make the day special.

They may use colourful decoration, very nice food and games and music to make the day special.

Your birthday is an important day each year.

Do you remember what happened on your birthday?

Did your family celebrate it?

Christian family celebrations

Christians have many important days.

Many families celebrate these each year.

They may have special food, parties and ceremonies on these days.

You may know the names of some Christian celebrations.

Let's learn about two of them.

One is called **Christmas**.

The other is called **Easter**.

Christmas

Christmas is all about a birthday.

It is the day when Christians celebrate the birth of Jesus Christ.

Jesus was born nearly 2,000 years ago and that is a very, very long time ago.

Christians celebrate the birthday of Jesus on the 25th of December each year.

This day is called **Christmas Day**.

In many countries Christmas Day is a holiday.

Do you remember what you did on Christmas Day?

Most people like to have a party when they celebrate a birthday.

Christians have parties at Christmas time.

Many of them have a lot of their favourite food and drink at their parties. They decorate their homes with streamers, balloons, coloured lights and other pretty things. They ask their relatives and friends to come to their Christmas parties. They may play games, sing songs and dance.

Christmas parties are happy times.

Christians are happy at Christmas because it is Jesus Christ's birthday. A Christmas party is one way to show how important Jesus is to all Christians.

Christmas presents

Most people like to give presents when it's someone's birthday.

Christians give presents to people at Christmas.

Many boys and girls hang stockings or pillow cases near their beds the night before Christmas. All kinds of nice things are found in them in the morning.

Perhaps you do this. Do you wonder where they all come from?

Many Christians act out a story about Santa Claus at Christmas. People dress up in a red and white costume and give presents to others. This reminds them of a story about a kind Christian man who gave presents at Christmas time.

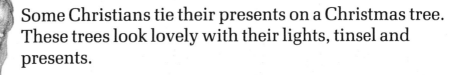

Some Christians tie their presents on a Christmas tree. These trees look lovely with their lights, tinsel and presents.

Some Christians go without presents and parties at Christmas. They prefer to give money, food and other things to help poor people.

Giving presents and helping other people can make people happy. Christmas is a special time for giving and receiving presents.

It is a happy time. For Christians, it is the celebration of Jesus Christ's birthday.

Christmas worship

Most Christian families like to go to church on Christmas Day. Many Christian families also worship in their homes at Christmas.

All the prayers, Bible readings, rituals and hymns used at Christmas help to tell the story of Jesus's birth.

Some families have little models dressed up like the people in the story of Jesus's birth. These will be on a table or sideboard for everybody to see.

Do you know this Christmas story?

The story is in three parts.

One is about a woman called Mary and a man called Joseph going to Bethlehem where Jesus was born.

The second is about some shepherds who heard about Jesus in a strange way.

The last part is about men who followed a star and found the baby Jesus in the town of Bethlehem.

The Christmas story

Mary and Joseph

Mary and Joseph had to travel a very long way. They were going to the town of Bethlehem.

The journey was very slow because they had to ride on a donkey.

Joseph cared for Mary, because she would soon have a little baby.

When they got to Bethlehem there was no room for them at the inn where they wanted to stay.

They had to sleep out in the stable where the animals lived.

That night, Mary had a little baby boy. She wrapped him up in warm clothes and put him in a manger to sleep.

Mary and Joseph called the baby Jesus. They looked after him. They fed him and kept him clean and warm.

Mary and Joseph knew that their little baby was very special.

The shepherds find Jesus

Some shepherds were out in a field not far from the stable. It was night and they were looking after their sheep.

Suddenly they saw an angel. The shepherds were frightened.

The angel told them not to be afraid. He had some good news to tell them.

> *'Jesus was born today in Bethlehem,' he said.*
> *'Go into Bethlehem and you will find the baby Jesus lying in a manger.'*

Soon there were lots of angels. They were all singing a beautiful hymn.

> *'Glory to God in the highest heaven,*
> *and peace on earth to those with whom he is pleased!'*

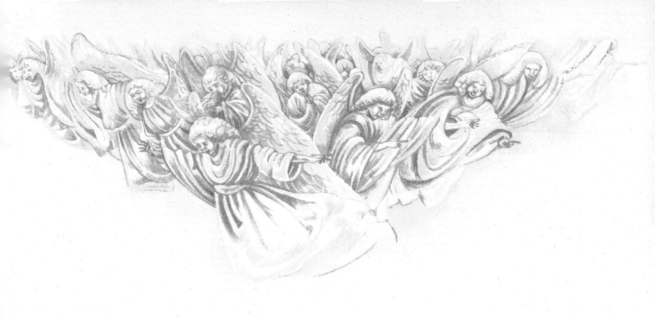

Now the shepherds knew that Jesus was someone very special.

They hurried to the stable and found the baby with Mary and Joseph.

Mary and Joseph were surprised when they heard about the angels.

Mary was very happy and wondered about her very special little baby.

Following a star

Wise men were also looking for Jesus.

They had seen a new star and had watched it for a long time.

The star led them to the stable in Bethlehem.

When they found the baby they were sure that he was someone very special. They believed that he was a new and famous king.

The wise men had brought presents for the new baby king.

They knelt down in front of the baby and gave him their presents.

These were very valuable gifts. There was gold, and two expensive perfumes called frankincense and myrrh.

The wise men were happy that they had found Jesus and given him their gifts. Then they set off on their long journey home.

Easter

What do you know about Easter?

Some of the pictures below are about Easter.

Some are not about Easter.

Look at each line of pictures and find the odd one out.

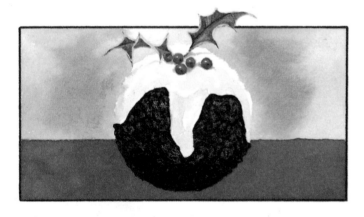 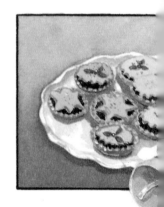

The odd ones out were about Easter.

Easter is different from Christmas.

Christmas is about Jesus being born.

Easter is about Jesus being killed and coming alive again.

Christmas is about cakes, puddings and lovely food.

Easter is about eggs, hot cross buns and plain food.

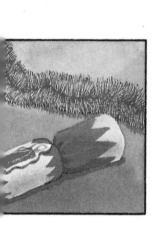

The Easter story

Jesus rides on a donkey

One day when Jesus was a grown up man, he decided to visit the city of Jerusalem.

He told his friends that he wanted to ride a donkey into the city.

'Why does he want to ride on a donkey?' thought his friends.

They didn't argue with him. They did what he said and found a donkey.

Crowds of people gathered to see Jesus. They had heard a lot about him and they wanted to see him.

Some people said that he was a very good teacher.
Others said that he could make sick people well.
Others said that he was their new king.
Some said that he was God's son.

There was a great deal of excitement as Jesus rode into the city.

Some people put their coats on the ground for the donkey to walk on. Others cut branches from the palm trees to spread in front of the donkey. Some remembered some lines from one of their old poems:

> *Look your king is coming to you!*
> *He is humble and rides on a donkey.*

'Oh!' thought his friends. 'That's why Jesus wanted to ride on a donkey. Perhaps he is telling us that he is our king. This made them shout and sing a lot louder.

There were some people who didn't like this at all.

They didn't like some of the things Jesus said.
They didn't like some of the things Jesus did.
They didn't like people saying that he was a king.
They didn't like people saying that he was God's son.
They became very angry.

Palm Sunday

Christians remember this part of the Easter story on Palm Sunday. If you listen to the story again, you may guess why Christians call this day Palm Sunday.

Palm Sunday is the first day of the Easter celebrations. These Easter rituals and worship last for a whole week.

Many Christian families go to church on Palm Sunday.

The story of Jesus riding into Jerusalem is an important part of the worship of this day.

Many Christians arc given a small cross made out of dried palm leaves to take home after the Palm Sunday worship. They may keep these in their Bibles or display them somewhere in the house. These crosses remind them of this part of the story. They also prepare them for the second part of the story.

Sometimes children may act out the story. They love to dress up and join in this play. Sometimes they dress up as a donkey. Sometimes a real donkey is used. Children and grown-ups like this.

Jesus is killed

Soon after his visit to the city of Jerusalem, Jesus went to a garden to pray.

One of his friends named Judas came to the garden with some soldiers.

Judas had betrayed Jesus to his enemies. He showed them where he was.

The soldiers took Jesus to the chief priest.

The chief priest asked Jesus, 'Are you God's son?' Jesus said, 'I am.'

'He says he is God's son. Nobody should say that. He is a liar. He must die,' said the chief priest.

Jesus was then taken away. He was beaten with a whip. The soldiers dressed him up like a king and made fun of him.

Some people called out, 'Nail him to a cross and let him die.'

The soldiers put a crown made of sharp thorns on his head.

Then they took Jesus to a hill near the city.

There they nailed Jesus to a cross made out of wood.

One of Jesus's best friends, John, was standing near to the cross. Jesus's mother Mary was there too.

Jesus said, 'John, look after my mother. Mother, take care of John.'

Jesus then looked at his enemies. He spoke to God and said, 'Father, forgive them. They don't understand what they are doing.'

Then Jesus bowed his head and died.

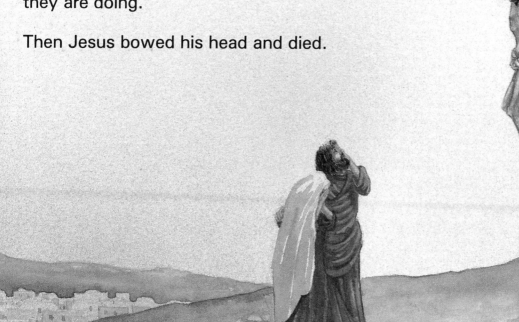

Christians remember this sad story on Good Friday.

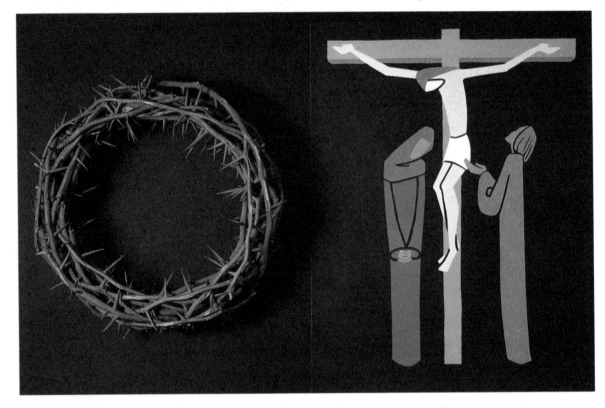

They believe that it is a good story.
They believe that Jesus was a good man and God's son.
They believe that this story shows how much Jesus loves
all people.

That's why Christians call this day Good Friday.

In many countries Good Friday is a holiday.

Many Christian families celebrate this day by going to
church. Some spend most of the day at church. Others go
to church and then have a rest, go on a picnic, visit
friends or do something else that they enjoy.

There are lots of other things that Christian families do to make Good Friday special.
Many Christians eat sweet buns with pastry crosses on them.
These are called hot cross buns.
Some go without food for the whole day.
Some do not eat meat on Good Friday.

Some give money away to help poor and hungry people.

Christians do these things on Good Friday to help them remember the story of Jesus being killed. For Christians this is a sad, but a good story.

The next part of the story is mysterious and happy. It will also help us to understand why Christians call the day on which Jesus was killed Good Friday.

Strange and mysterious happenings

Jesus's friends took his body down from the cross. They put it in a cave and rolled a big stone in front of the entrance. It was late on Friday afternoon.

On Sunday morning some of Jesus's friends went to the cave. The large stone was rolled away.

Jesus wasn't there! An angel was there.

The angel said, 'Jesus is alive. Go and tell all his friends.'

Later that day, two men were walking to a town called Emmaus. They were friends of Jesus and were very sad. They had not heard that Jesus was alive.

A man joined them on the walk. He talked to them about Jesus.

When they arrived at Emmaus, the two men asked the stranger to come and eat with them.

During the meal the stranger said thank you to God for the food. This was just like the way Jesus used to do it. Then the men knew that this was Jesus.

Back in Jerusalem, the other friends of Jesus were sad and frightened. They were hiding in a little room. Suddenly Jesus was in the room with them. He told them not to be frightened. Then he shared some food with them.

'It is Jesus!' they said. 'He is alive.'

Then Jesus disappeared from their sight.

Easter Sunday

Christians remember this part of the story on Easter Sunday.

Easter Sunday is the last day of the Easter celebrations. It is the most important day of the year for Christians.

All their worship and rituals on Easter Sunday tell this strange and mysterious story. These celebrations are full of joy because of what Christians believe.

They believe that Jesus was killed on the cross.
They believe that Jesus came back to life again.
They believe that Jesus is everywhere, even though no one can see him.

Some Christian families stay up very late on the night before Easter Sunday. At midnight they go to their church so that they can worship as soon as Easter Sunday begins.

Some Christians get up very early in the morning on Easter Sunday. They get out of bed while it is still very dark. They meet other Christians in a park or out on a hill. As the sun rises they worship God and remember the mystery of Jesus coming back to life again.

Many Christians give each other Easter eggs on this special day. The eggs may be made of chocolate or other sweets. Some people boil ordinary eggs and paint lovely, colourful patterns on them.

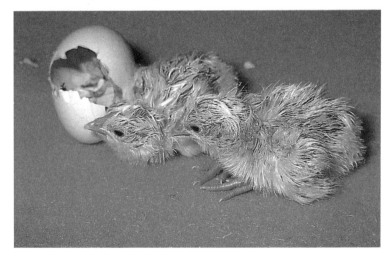

Have you ever seen a little chicken coming out of an egg?

If you have, you may guess why Christians like giving colourful Easter eggs to each other on Easter Day.

Have you ever seen the sun rise?

If you have, you may guess why some Christians like to think of this story as they watch the sunrise.

Notes for teachers

The material in this book is intended to help very young children learn about Christians. Christian practices and beliefs are described clearly and without apology. However, this is done without any assumptions being made about any teacher's or pupil's acceptance of the Christian religion now or in the future.

This book is the first in a series of four books. It is designed for the 5–8 (lower primary) age group. It is therefore intended to contribute to the first three years of the child's R.E. in school.

There are two parts to this book. Part One introduces children to some of the important features of Christian communities. In Part Two they learn about aspects of Christian family life. The Christian community is dealt with first so that children have some idea of basic Christian beliefs and practices before they consider the specifically religious aspects of Christian family life. The two parts are indicated by colour coding: pink for Part One and blue for Part Two. The coloured box round each page number shows which part the page is in.

There is a wide range of language difficulty within the book. The easier passages may be read by younger children. The harder passages may be read by pupils who are keeping up with the level of language difficulty or they may be read by the teacher to less able pupils.

Several stories appear in this book. They have been printed in different type for easier identification. They can be read at any time to groups of any ability. The pictures accompanying the text may help younger pupils follow the story as it is read to them. Pupils at the top end of this age group may be able to read these stories themselves.

In this book pupils are introduced to several key words and concepts which are considered essential for their continuing religious education.

Human experience words: Communities, rituals, ceremonies, belonging, needing, sharing, caring.

General religious words: God, prayer, worship, belief.

Christian words: Christians, Jesus Christ, Bible, church, ministers, priests, Holy Communion, baptism, dedication and thanksgiving, Christmas, Palm Sunday, Good Friday, Easter Sunday, altar, font, pulpit, lectern, paten, chalice.

Content overview of the pupils' books

The four pupils' books in this series are designed to help pupils develop an understanding of Christianity as a world religion. Each book deals with different aspects of Christian practices, beliefs and experiences.

The diagrammatic presentation below indicates the content of each book and shows how children are helped to build up, in a progressive way from 5–16, their knowledge and understanding of this religion. The shaded areas in the circles indicate the aspects of Christianity dealt with in particular books.

A more detailed explanation of this way of distributing the materials across the four books is given in the teacher's books, *How do I teach R.E.?* and *Christianity.*

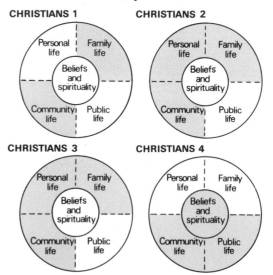

Other materials in this Project

Teachers using this book with lower primary children must realise that it is only one resource item designed to meet one specific aspect of the primary child's experience of R.E. – learning about Christians, through the words and concepts outlined above. To expand the range of classroom activities designed to meet this need, a **photopack**, with additional pictures and information, is also available.

Teachers using these resources are strongly recommended to refer to the two teacher's books: *How do I teach R.E.?* – the main Project manual *Christianity* – a source book and guide to the teaching of this religion.

Books and photopacks relating to other religious traditions are also part of **The Westhill Project: R.E. 5–16.**